O9-BTO-662

Being
Born

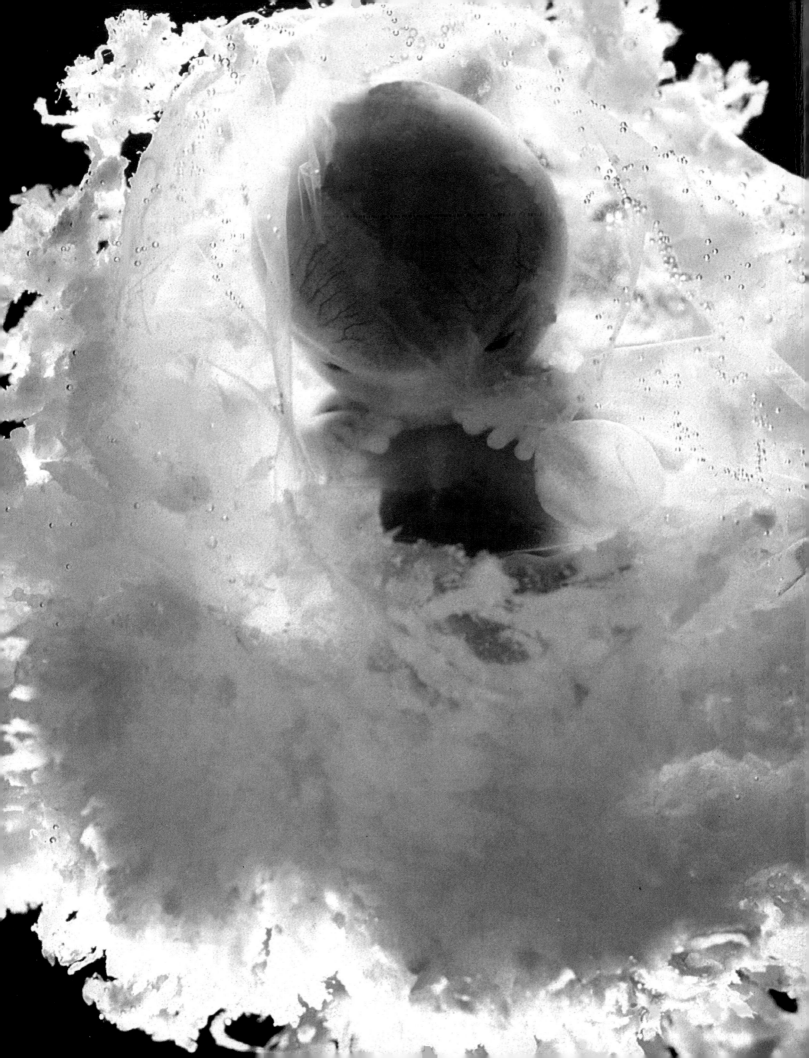

Being Born

Sheila Kitzinger

PHOTOGRAPHY BY
Lennart Nilsson

Grosset & Dunlap · New York

Designer: Tessa Richardson-Jones
Art Director: Roger Bristow

Managing Editor: Jackie Douglas
Editorial Director: Christopher Davis

First published in the United States in 1986
by Grosset & Dunlap, a member of
The Putnam Publishing Group, New York

Library of Congress Catalog Card Number: 86-080513

ISBN 0-448-18990-9

Color reproduction by F. E. Burman, Ltd.
Type set by MS Filmsetting Limited, Frome, Somerset.
Printed in Italy by A. Mondadori Editore, Verona.

C D E F G H I J

A NOTE TO THE READER SHARING THIS BOOK WITH A CHILD

These pages record the unfolding of a journey which each of us
has taken, but of which we have only momentary glimpses, or
cannot remember at all.

It is not the story of what happens when a baby brother or sister is
born, but about what a child could see, hear, feel and do deep inside
the mother's body, and about the *baby's* experience of birth.

For a mother and her child, pregnancy is the time when they are in
the closest partnership, intimately joined together in an experience
which is rarely discussed, and often forgotten.

In these pages all that can be learned from prenatal psychologists,
ultrasound, and electronic recording of the fetal heart is combined to
retrace that adventure of the nine months of prenatal life.

Sheila Kitzinger
Lennart Nilsson

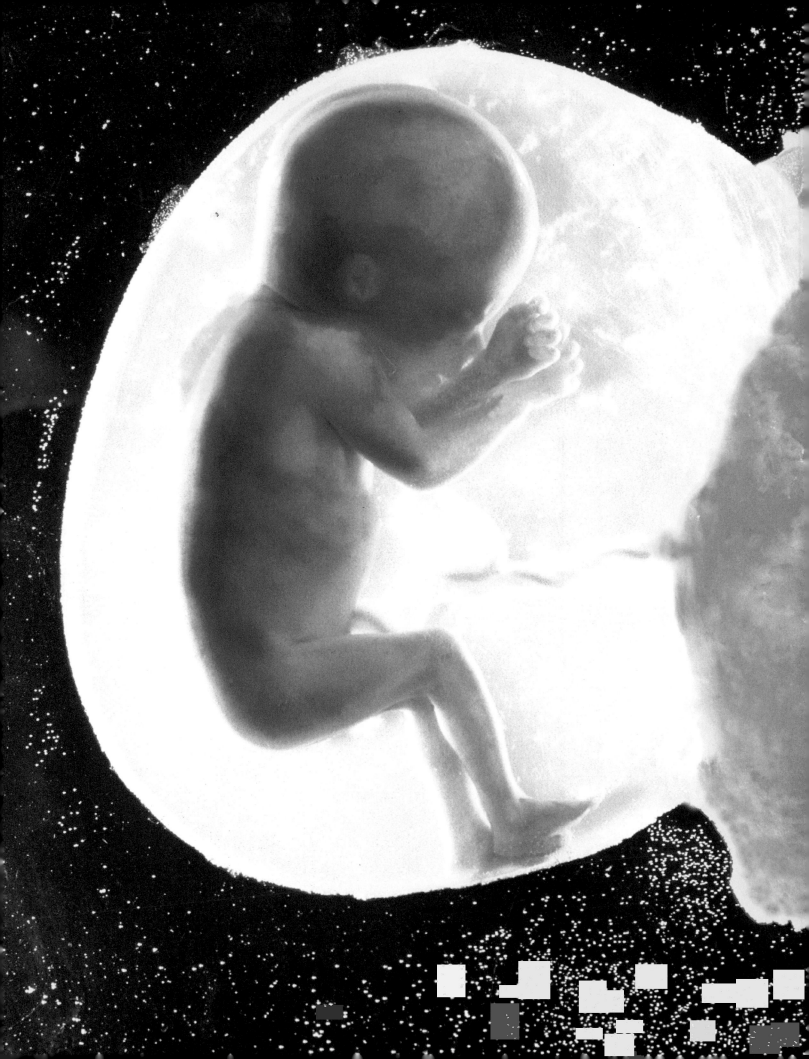

Once you were in a small, dark place inside your mother's body,
floating in a balloon of warm water.
It was your mother's uterus.
The walls of the uterus were firm and springy.

They were made of muscle—
like the muscles in your arms which get hard
when you pull
or push,
and the muscles in your legs which get hard
when you climb
or run.

You didn't need to breathe air.
Instead, blood flowed through a tube
to the middle of your belly,
around your body, and out through the tube again.
Good things from your mother's blood—
from the food she ate and the air she breathed—
passed straight into your blood.
She ate and drank for you.
She breathed for you.

You did not know you were you.
You did not know where you were.
Like a seed beginning to grow in the earth,
which does not realize that it will be a flower,
you were growing inside your mother.

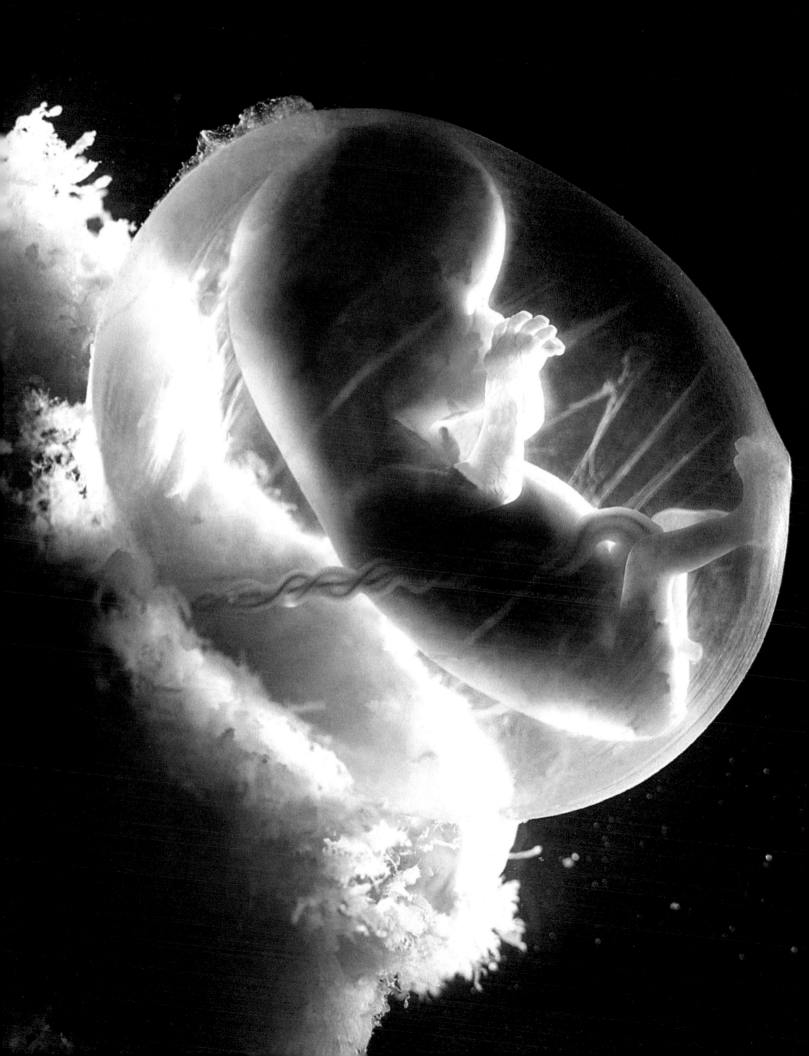

At the very beginning there was no you.
Like a seed in a soft round pod,
a tiny egg
lay in an ovary deep inside
your mother's body.
The egg was as small as this period.
It was called an ovum.
The ovum was packed with food and energy to make a baby.
When the ovum was ripe it started to move
into a tube that arches between the ovary and your mother's uterus.
It was going on a very long journey—
one which took three days and nights
and sometimes longer still—
along the tube and into the uterus.
As the ovum moved, other cells clustered around it
like a swarm of bees, helping to feed it.

But the ovum needed something else
before it could grow into a baby.
It needed sperm before you could start growing.
Millions of sperm, much smaller than the ovum,
were in the testicles behind your father's penis.
When your mother and father felt very loving,
they kissed and cuddled each other.
Your father's penis became hard so that it could slide
into your mother's vagina,
the soft opening between her legs
which leads to her uterus.
As your mother and father held each other in their arms,
a liquid called semen
spurted out from his penis into her vagina.

The semen was full of tiny sperm
so small that no one could see them.
They shot out and swam up the vagina,
through the uterus and into the tube
along which the ovum was traveling.
Many of the sperm got tired and gave up
or went the wrong way.
But others reached the ovum and crowded around it.
The wall of the ovum was soft.
One sperm burrowed into the wall of the ovum
and the ovum sucked it inside.
The sperm had joined with the ovum
to form one cell.

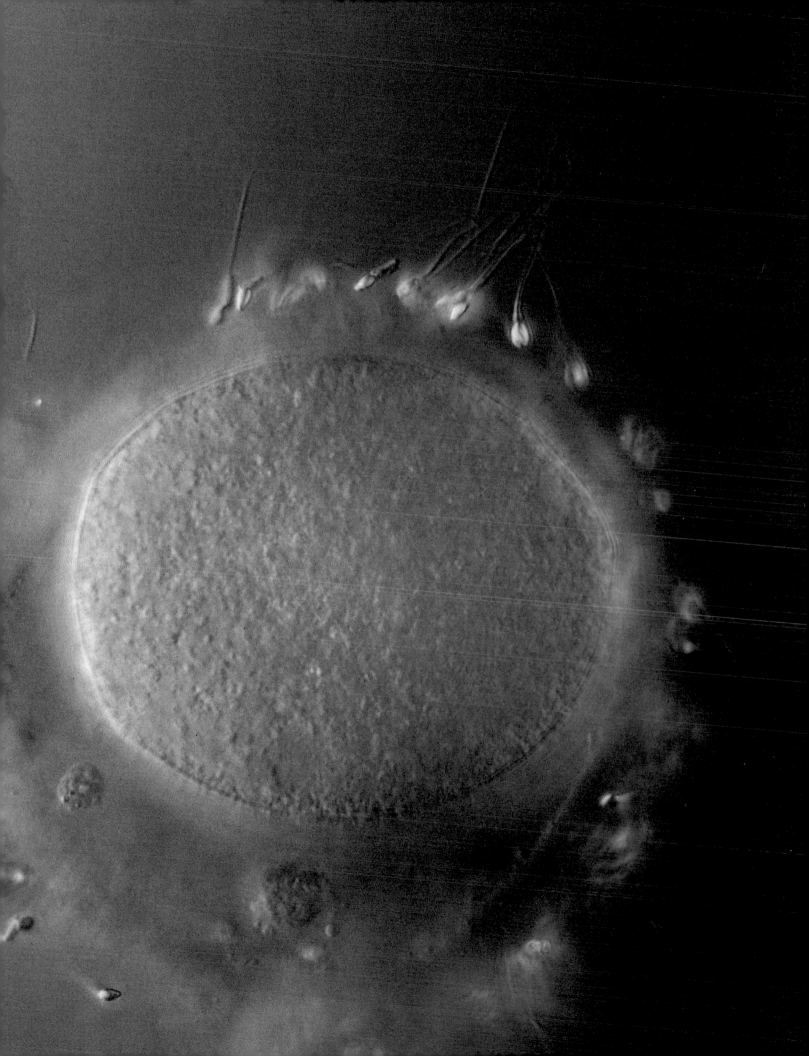

The one cell split into two cells.
The two cells split into four.
The four cells split into eight.

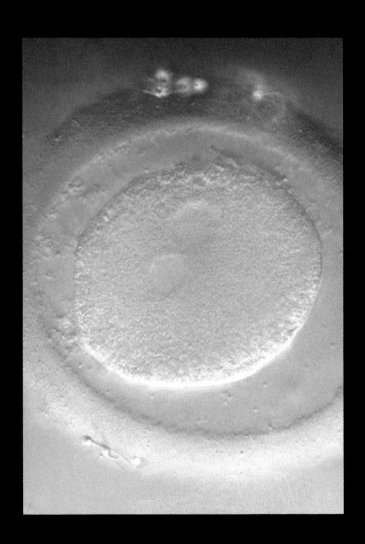

And the ball of cells grew and grew till it looked like a shimmering, silvery blackberry.

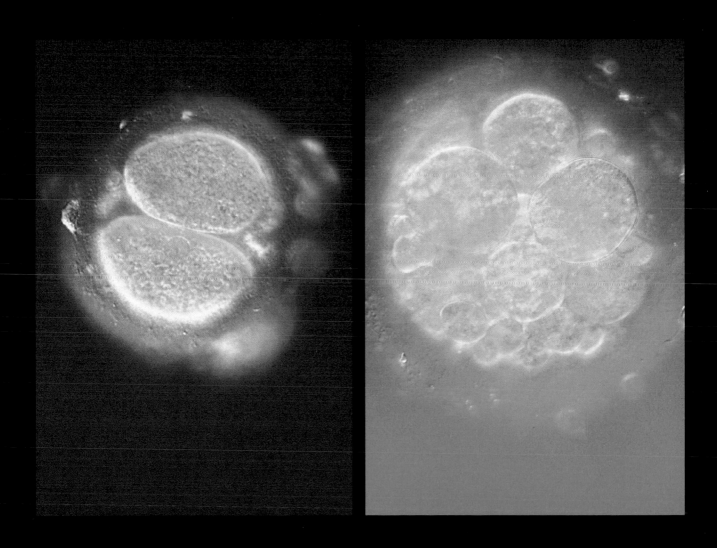

All the time the ball of cells was growing,
it moved along the tube toward the uterus.
It was bouncing like a tiny ball, getting bigger and bigger.

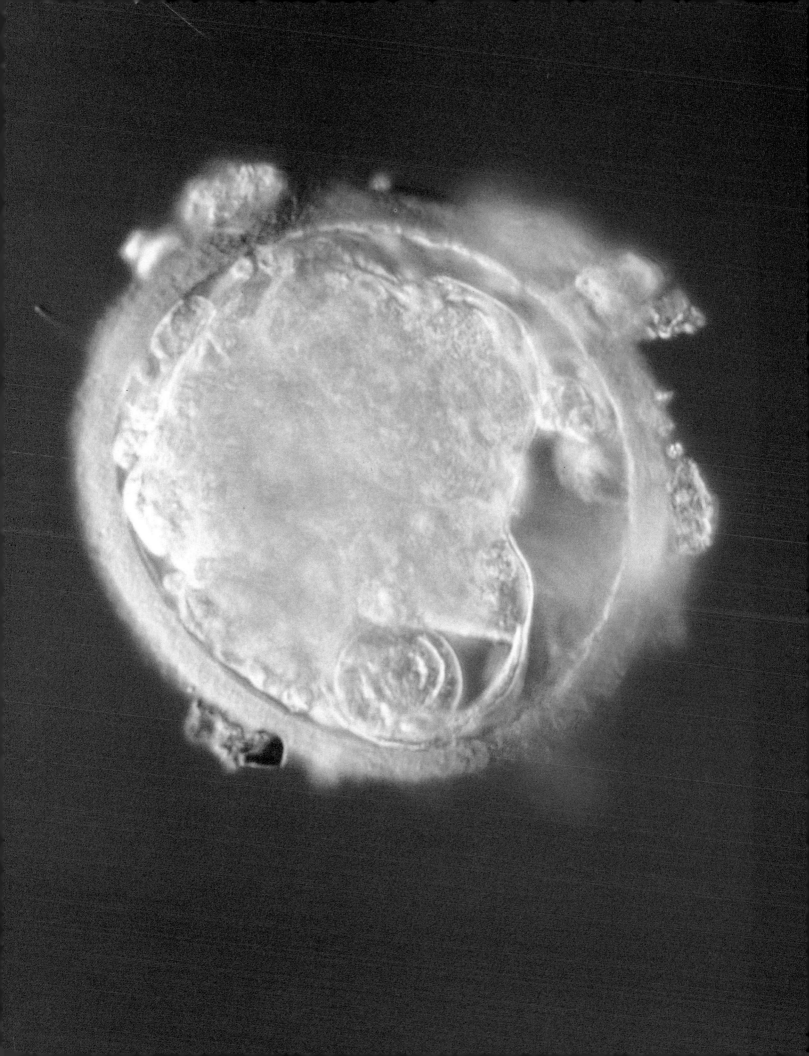

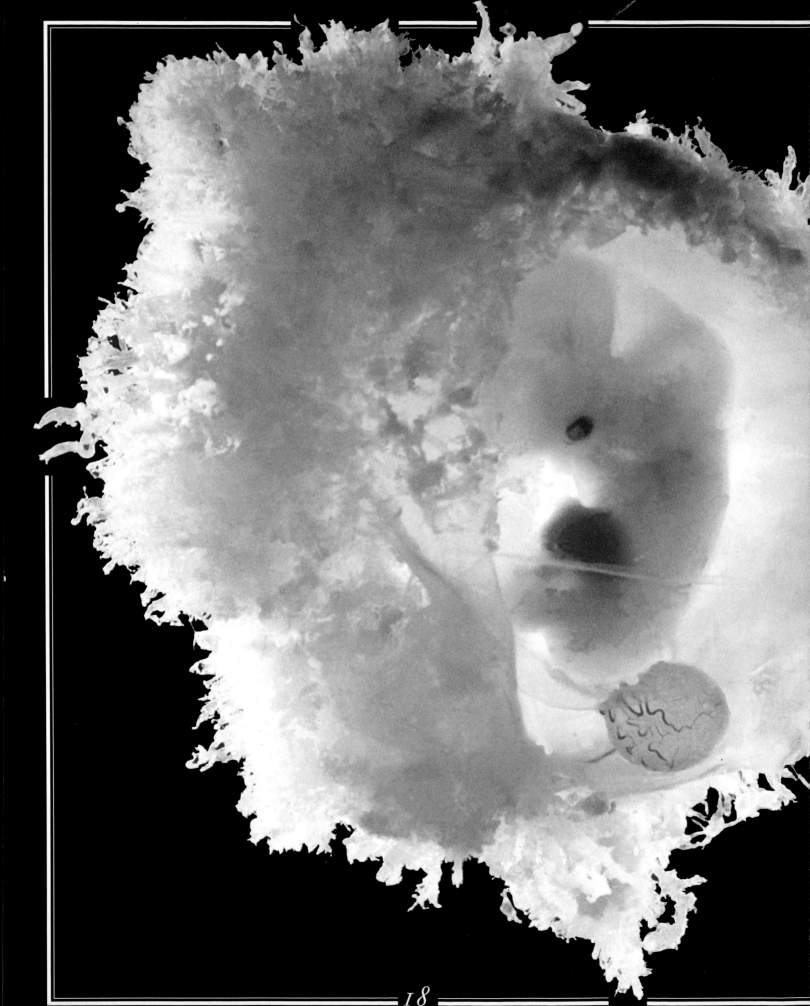

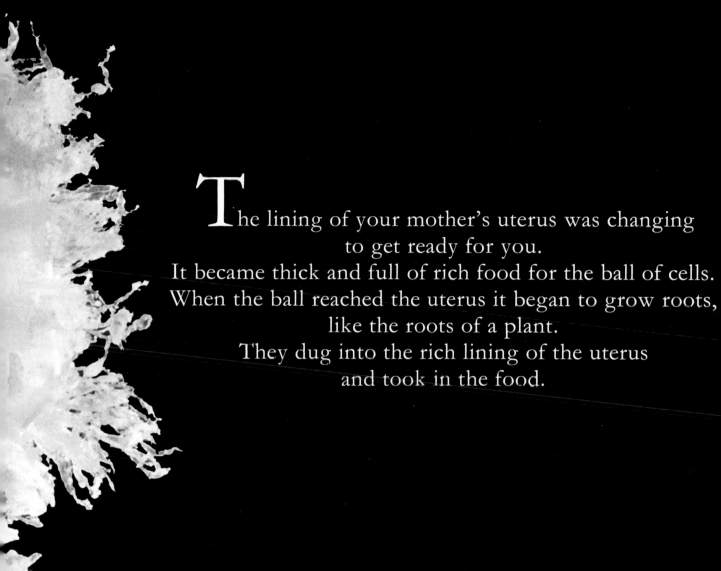

The lining of your mother's uterus was changing
to get ready for you.
It became thick and full of rich food for the ball of cells.
When the ball reached the uterus it began to grow roots,
like the roots of a plant.
They dug into the rich lining of the uterus
and took in the food.

The ball now had a top end,
big and round,
that was going to be your head,
and a bottom end that was thin and curved like a tail.
Your body began to grow from the back
and to join up at the front like a coat being zipped up.
One part of the cell ball started to grow
into a tree of thin tubes—a placenta—
through which blood could flow.

After 30 days you were 5 mm ($\frac{1}{5}$ inch) long.

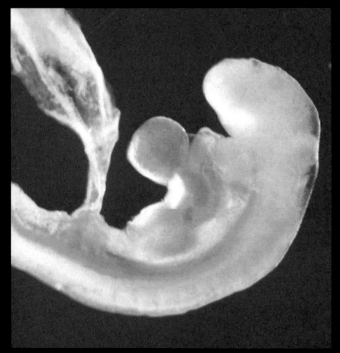
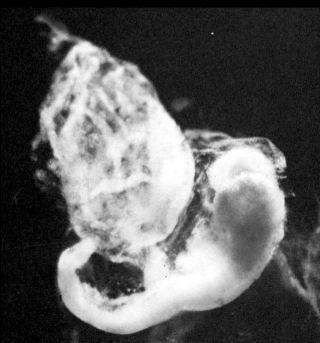

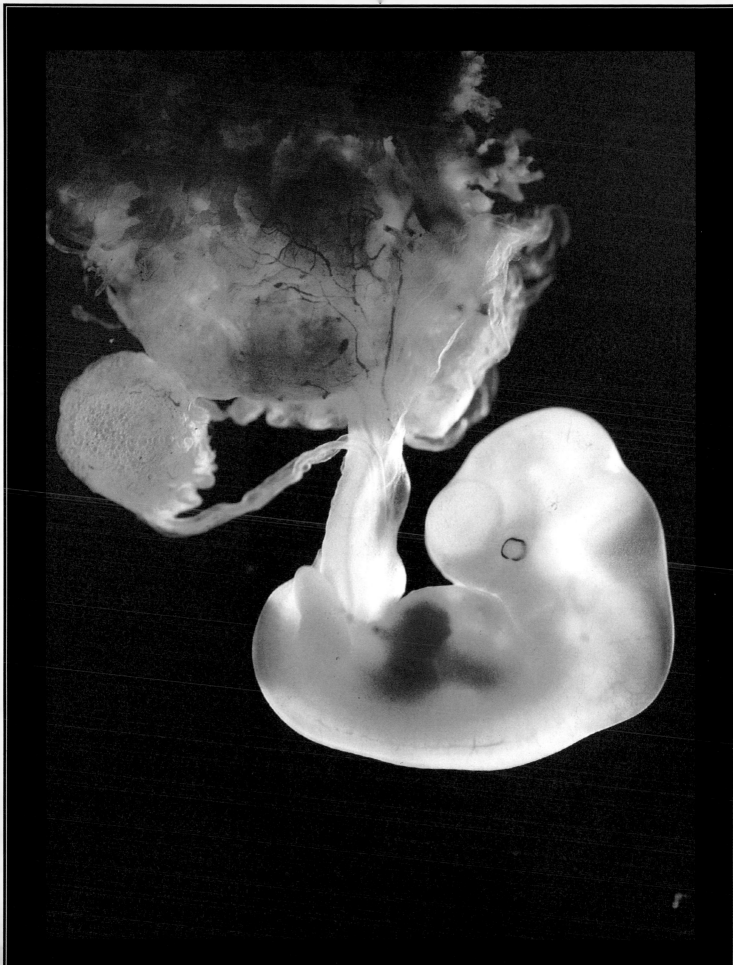

Y ou didn't look much like a baby yet—
more like a sprouting bean. . . .
And then, like a tiny sea-horse,
you grew little ridges down your back
that would later form your backbone.
Your skin was very thin, like tissue paper,
and under the skin your heart was beating.

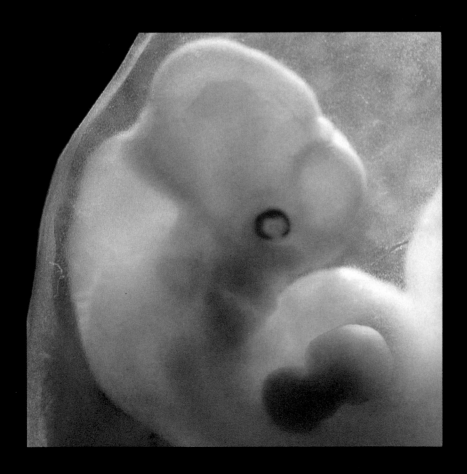

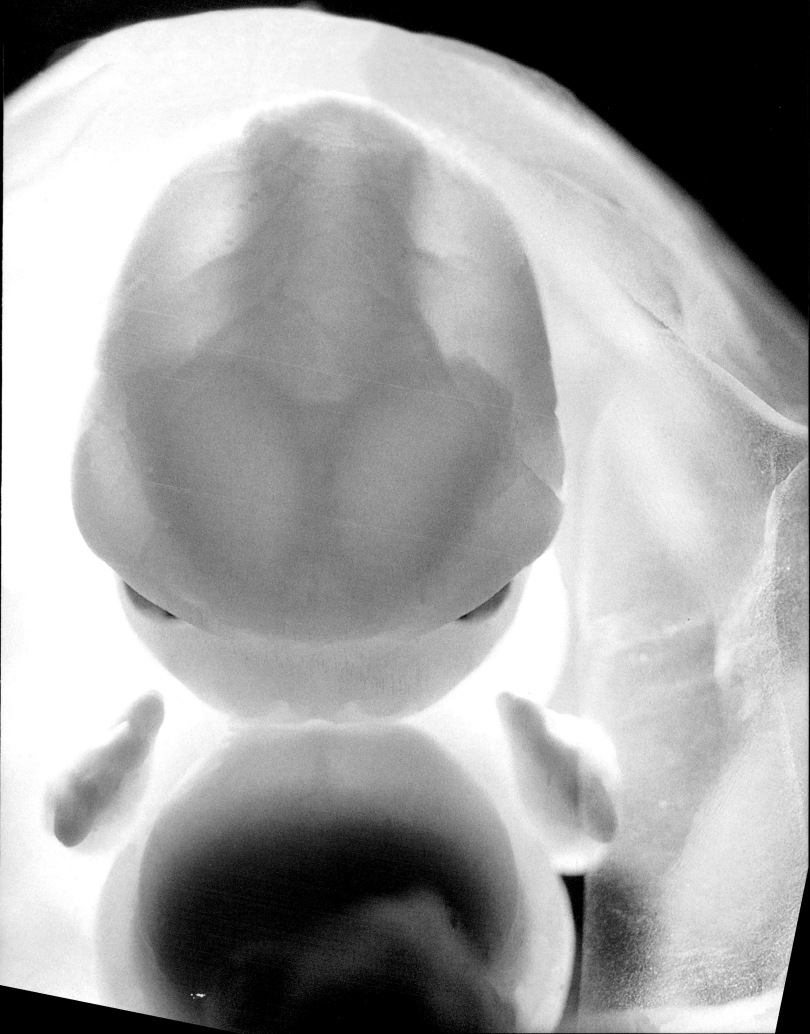

At five weeks your arms started to grow.
They looked like little sprouts.

After 5 weeks you were 12 mm (½ inch) long.

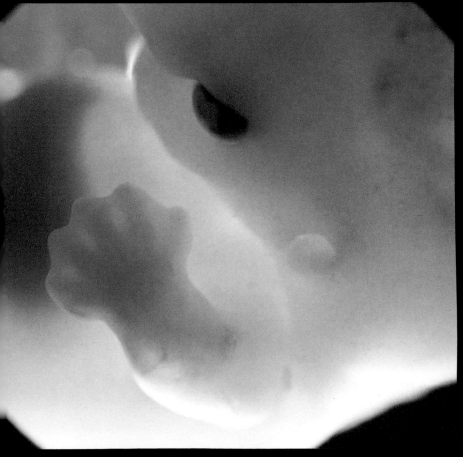

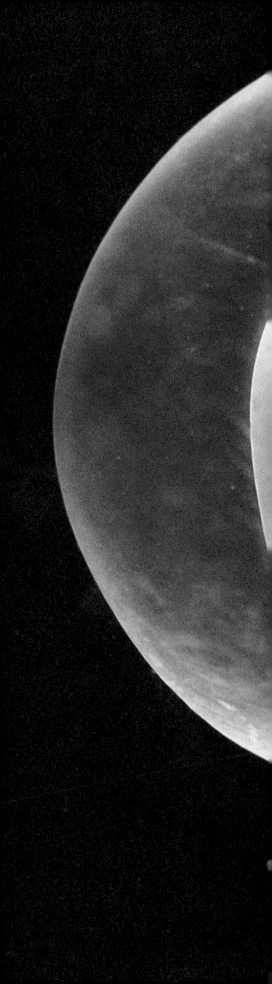

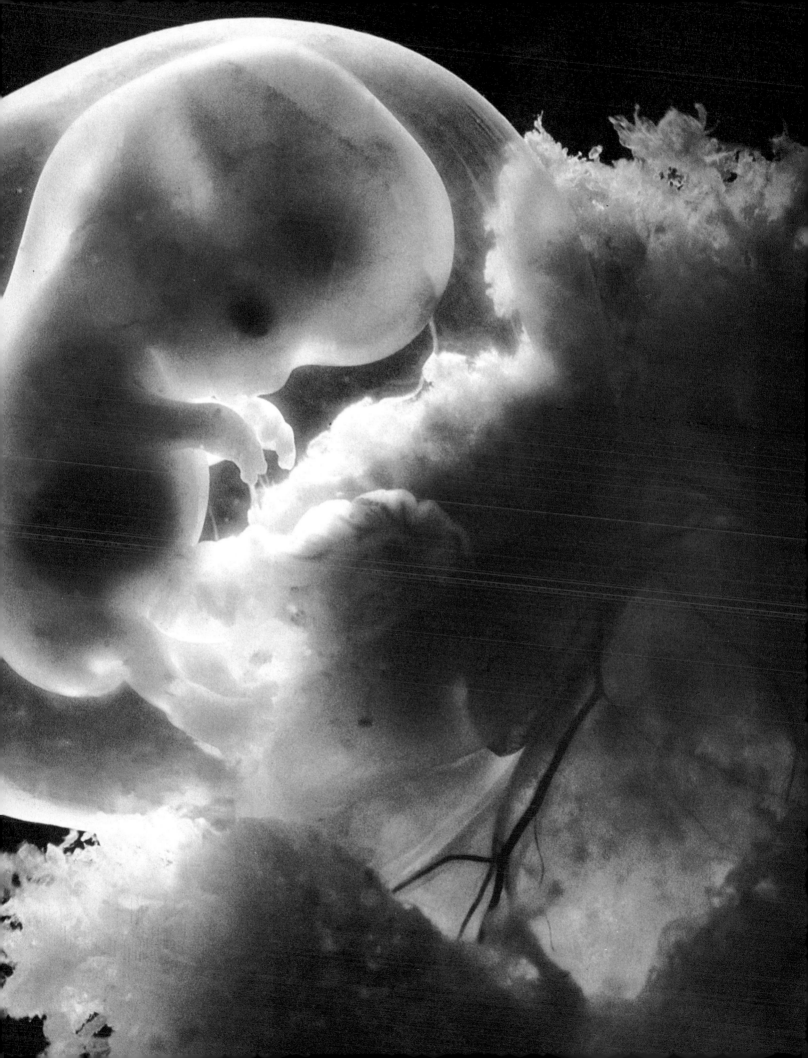

Nine or ten weeks after you had started to grow
you could open and close your mouth.
After twelve weeks you could make funny faces.
You could frown,
and press your lips together,
and push your lips forward.
Yet you still weighed only as much as
a hen's egg in its shell.

Your belly button or navel is the place
where there was a tube joining you to your placenta.
The tube was called the umbilical cord.
Blood full of oxygen
and nourishment from your mother's food
flowed through this cord from your mother into you.
All the blood came through your placenta.
It filtered through
as if through a strainer or a sieve.
Then it flowed into the cord that went into your belly.
It pulsed along the cord like water through a garden hose.

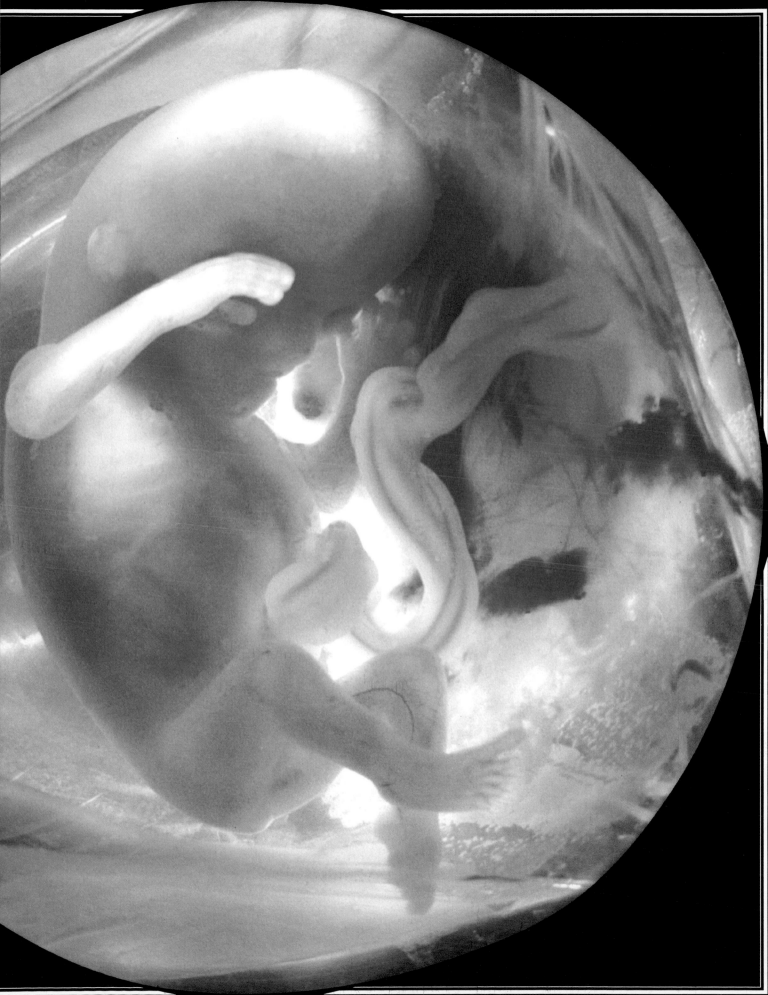

You had been growing for eleven weeks now.
Your legs and arms could move.
You stretched out your arms.
You kicked your feet.
It was easy to move because you were in a bubble of water.
You could swim like a fish.
But you were still so tiny
that your mother could not feel you moving.

After 11 weeks you were 5 cm (2 inches) long.

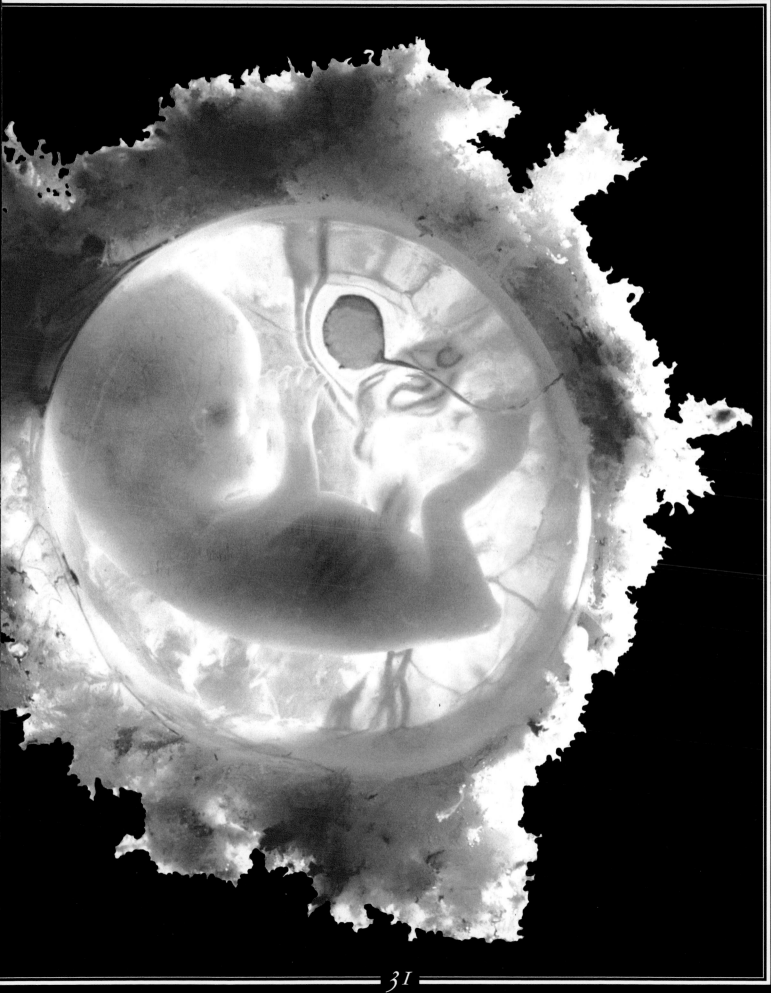

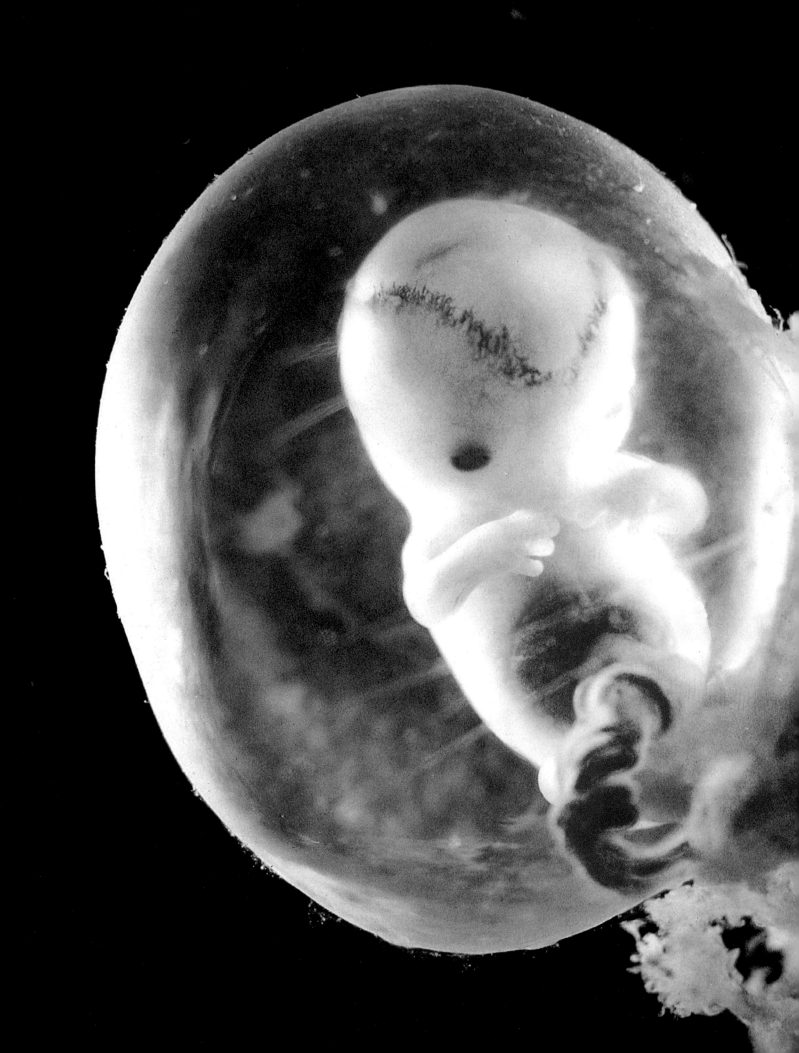

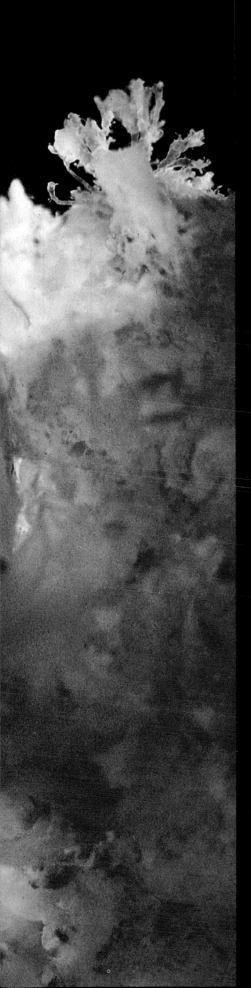

It was warm inside the uterus—
like being in a warm bath in a darkened room.
Fresh, warm water kept flowing in
to keep you comfortable.
It was quite fresh again every six hours.
It never got cold.
You were warm and curled up
and it felt just right.

Sometimes you drank the water in which you floated.
You sucked it in,
practicing the movements you would use to get milk
after you were born.

When you had been growing for about five months
your mother felt you move.
At first your kicks were faint,
like butterflies inside her,
or little fish swimming,
or soap bubbles that float and pop.

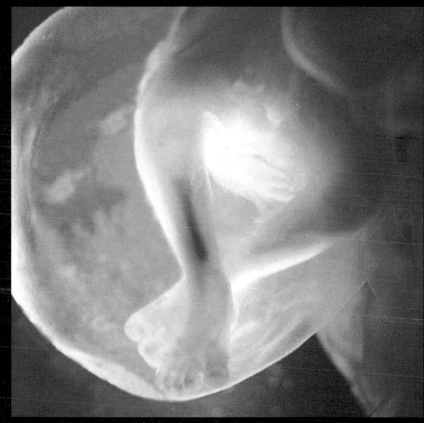

After 5 months you were 25 cm (10 inches) long.

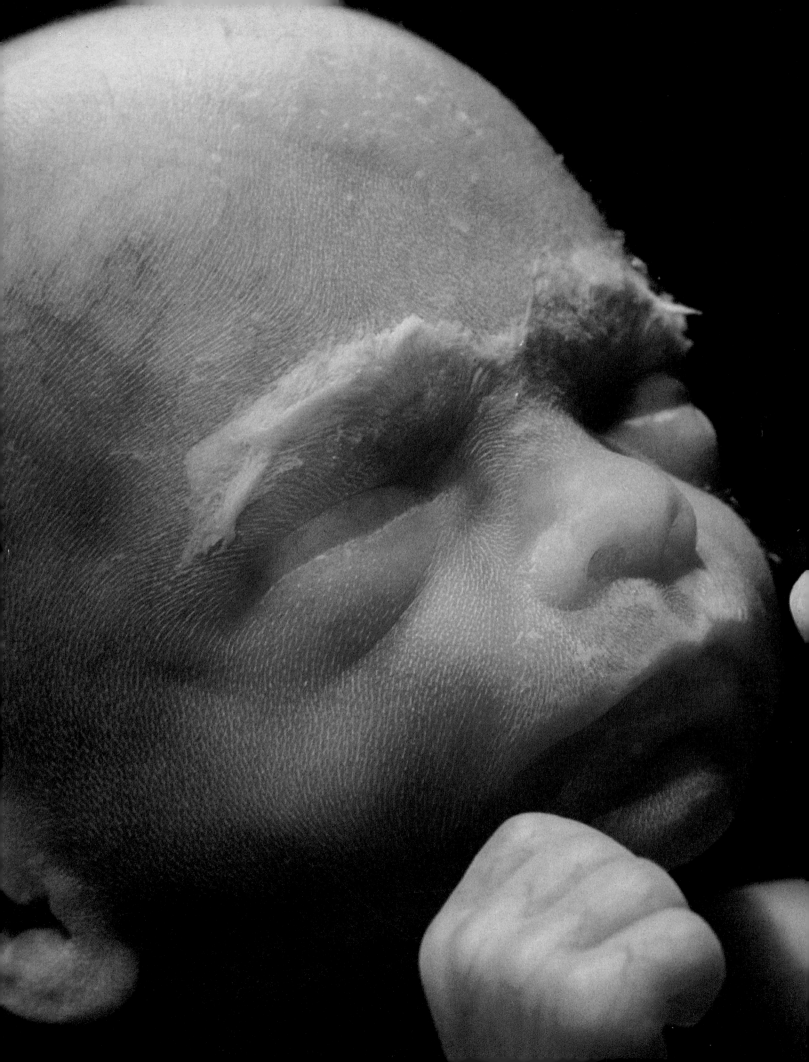

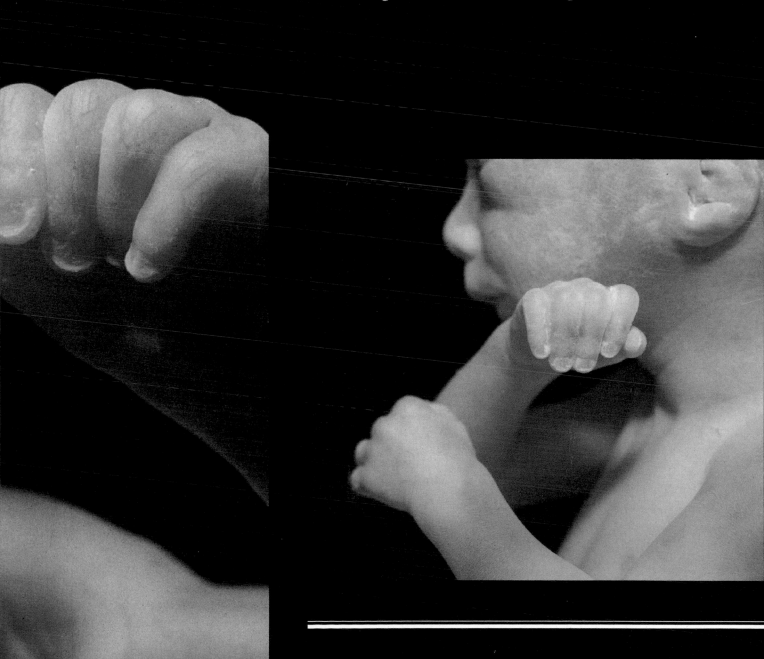

By now you could curl up your fingers
and close your hand
and make a fist
and punch.
When you were wide awake
your mother could feel you punch and kick,
flip from side to side,
and sometimes even turn somersaults.

Your skin had a white creamy coating
that kept it from wrinkling in the water.

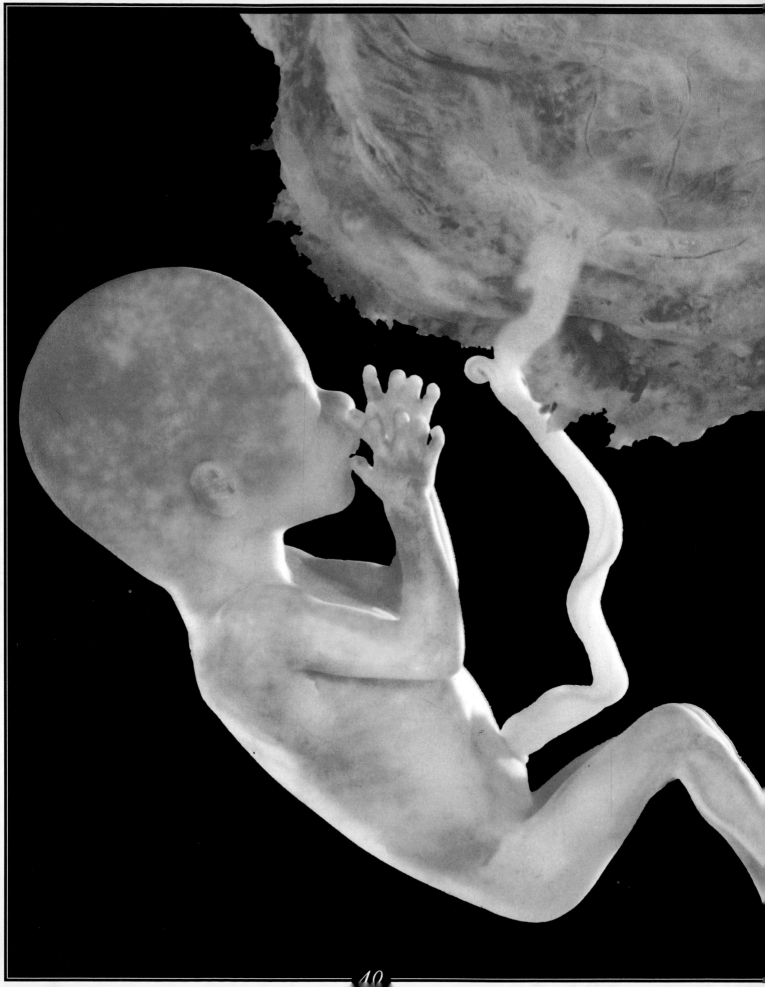

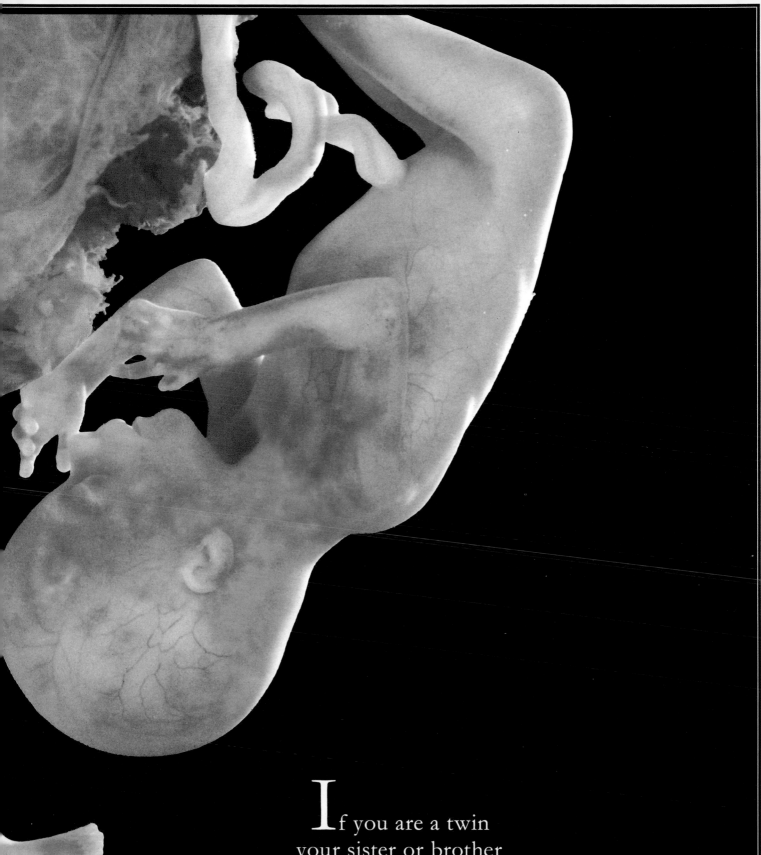

$$\mathrm{I}_{\text{f you are a twin}}$$
your sister or brother
grew with you, close together, inside your mother's body.
Sometimes there are three babies—triplets—
or even more.

Your fingers reached out and felt water.
Your fingers touched wet, shiny skin.
Your face felt the touch
and your fingers felt it too.
Then they slipped away again, into the water.
Your fingers were the first things you played with.
They moved like the fronds of a sea anemone in a rock pool.
Then one day your fingers found your mouth
and brushed your lips.
You liked the feeling
and you began to suck your hand.

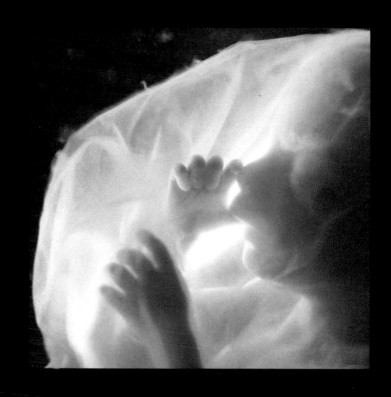

Gradually you learned how to bring your hand to your mouth.
And then, one day,
you popped your thumb in
and sucked it for the very first time.
You sucked very hard and drank in some water too.
You may have sucked so hard that you got hiccups.
Your mother could feel you go
bump—bump—bump.
If she didn't guess what had happened she may have been surprised
and wondered what you were doing.

As the weeks passed, you grew bigger.
You rolled into a tight ball,
your knees tucked up to your chin.
Your arms were crossed in front of you.
Your head was forward on your chest.
It was a tight fit.

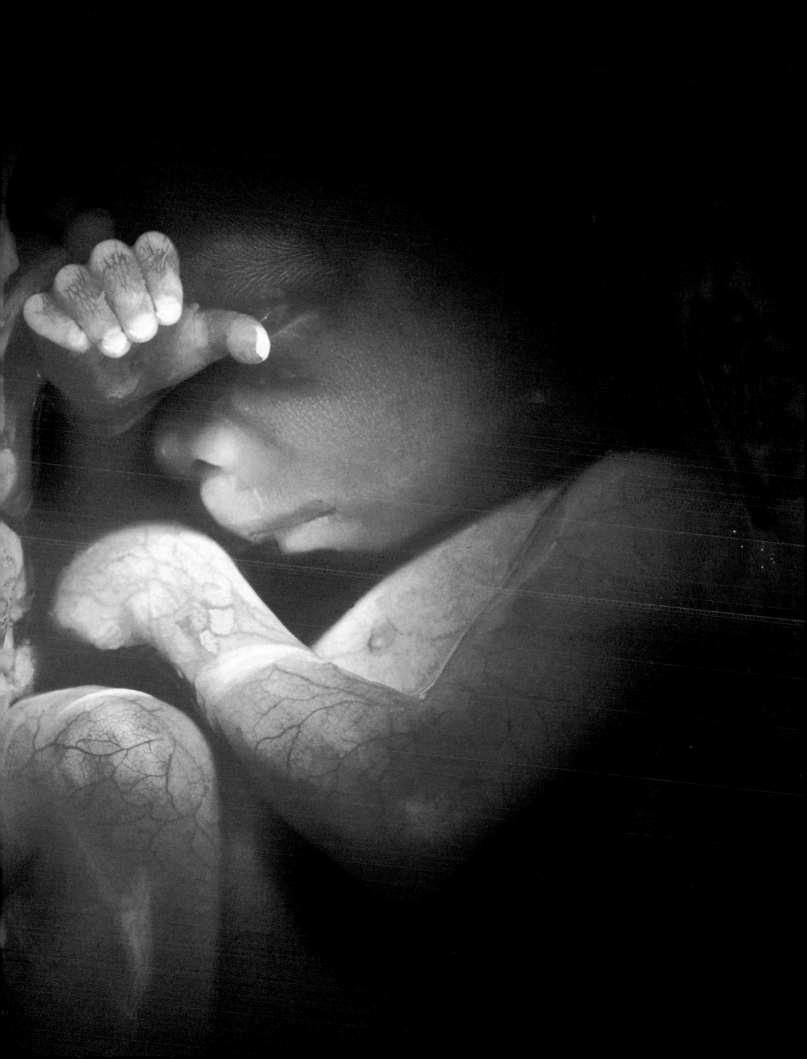

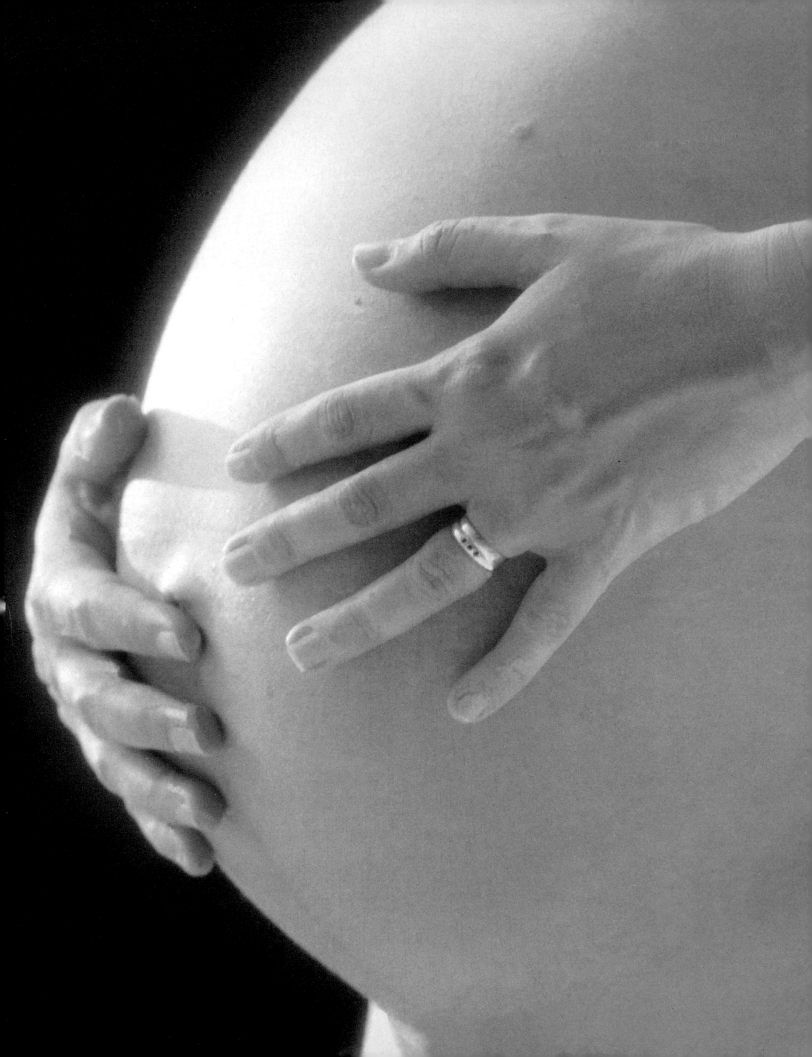

You grew and grew,
and your mother's belly got bigger
to make space for you.

When you had been inside your mother's body for six months
you could hear her voice.
Often when she spoke you moved,
almost as if you could talk to her with your whole body.
She spoke and you listened.
Then you moved.
She spoke again and you stayed still.
Then, when she had finished speaking, you would move again.
Loud bangs made you jump.

Sometimes you went to sleep for a long time.
Then, when your mother went to bed and was about to fall asleep,
you would wake up and bounce around.

After 6 months you were about 30 cm (12 inches) long.

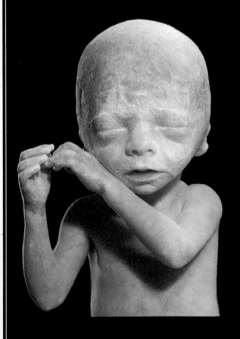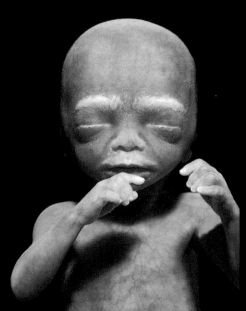

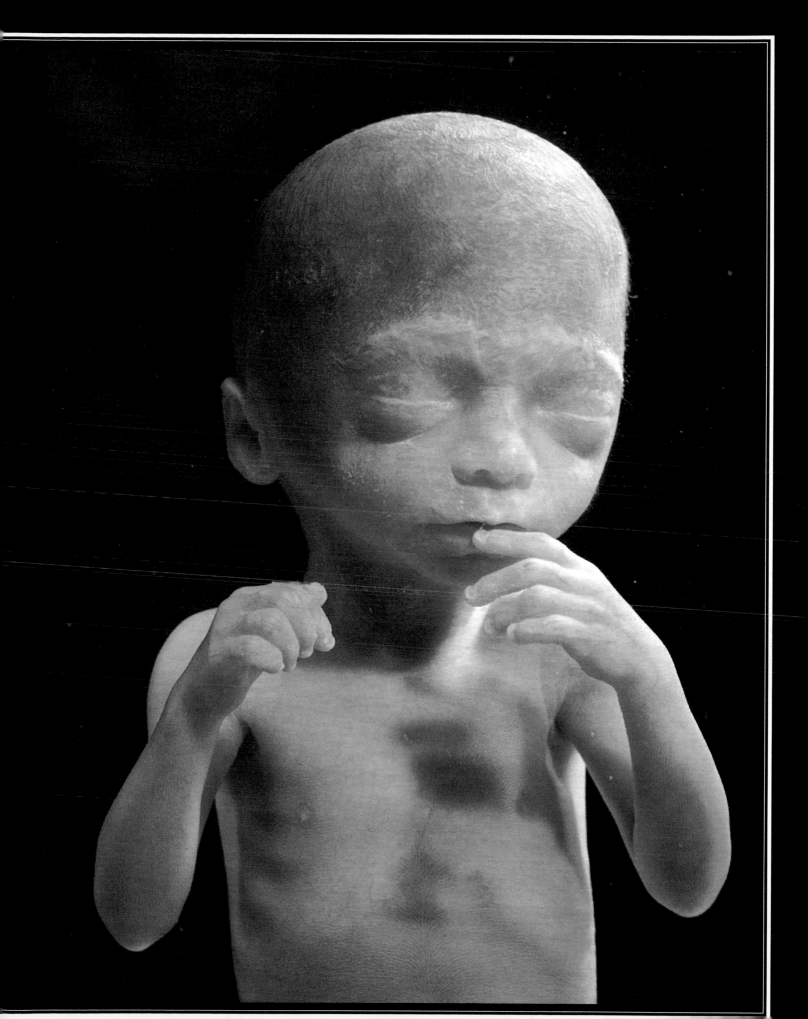

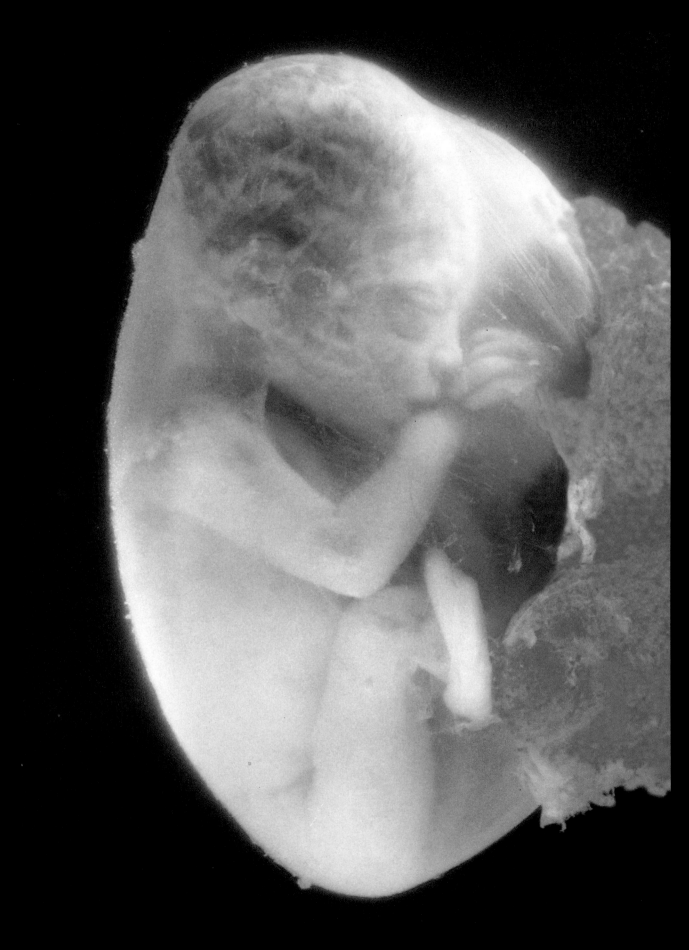

Sometimes other people could see you move.
A bump would shift from one side of your mother's belly to the other.
Was it your bottom?
Or your foot?
Or your knee?
Or your elbow?
Perhaps your mother guessed what it was.

You had been growing for seven months
and now you opened your eyes.
When a bright light shone near your mother's belly
it glowed through into the place where you were.
The bubble in which you lay was lit up with red light,
as if you were under a lamp with a crimson shade.

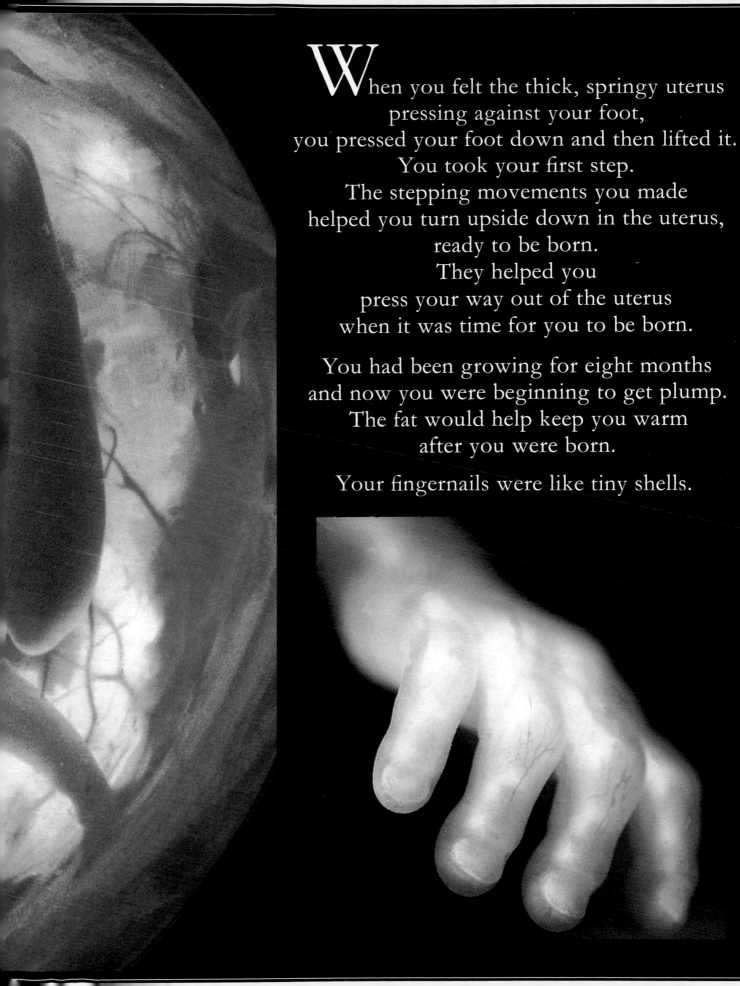

When you felt the thick, springy uterus
pressing against your foot,
you pressed your foot down and then lifted it.
You took your first step.
The stepping movements you made
helped you turn upside down in the uterus,
ready to be born.
They helped you
press your way out of the uterus
when it was time for you to be born.

You had been growing for eight months
and now you were beginning to get plump.
The fat would help keep you warm
after you were born.

Your fingernails were like tiny shells.

Soon you would be born.
You had been inside your mother all the time
from autumn, when the leaves were falling,
till summer, when the sun shone hot.
Or from summer till the next spring came
and birds built their nests.
Or from spring till winter,
when frost-patterns formed on the windowpane
and cold winds blew.
You weren't kicking much now because there was so little room.
Then one day—
or perhaps it was in the middle of the night—
your mother could feel her uterus tightening, hard,
and then relaxing.
She knew that you were ready to be born.
As the uterus tightened, its opening gradually got bigger,
and bigger,
and bigger,
until the top of your head could press through into her vagina,
in the same way that you push your head through a turtleneck
when you put one on.
Every time the uterus tightened it squeezed you.
It felt like a very big hug.

Then the bubble of water in which you lived popped
and—WHOOSH—out came the water.
Now you were squeezed even harder.
It felt like a big hand pushing against your bottom.
The soft walls of the vagina spread apart.
They opened wider and wider.
At last you reached an arch of bone
and your head dipped under it.
Your chin pressed against your chest,
as if you were crawling into a box
or under a bed.
When you had passed under the bone
you could raise your head,
and it felt as if a hand were holding you underneath your chin and
lifting it.
Your mother, if she were looking in a mirror,
could see a tiny bit of the top of your head in her vagina.
It looked like a wrinkled walnut,
dark and damp and glistening.
It inched forward a bit more
each time her uterus tightened.
Her vagina was stretched wide open
as the top of your head slid out.

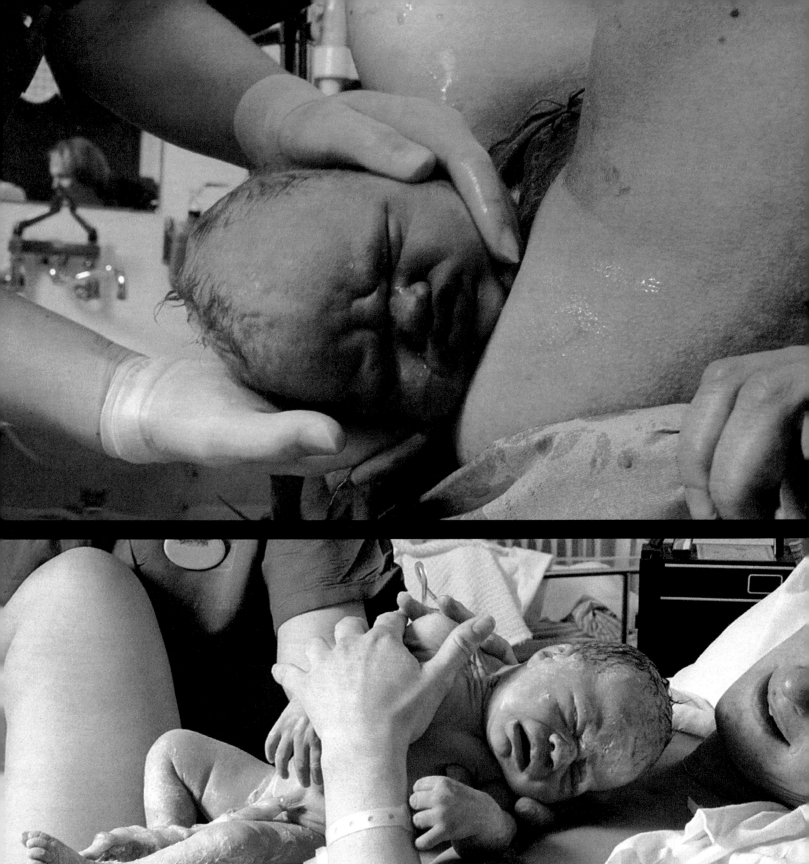

Then the rest of your head slipped out
and it turned,
and a shoulder slid out
and then the other,
and your chest
and you could breathe.
The rest of your body slithered out in a rush.
You could move
and cry.
You could open your eyes and see your mother
and hear her voice.

As you breathed,
air rushed in and out of your lungs.
Before you were born
your lungs were stuck together like empty plastic bags.
But when you took your first big breath,
they came unstuck and opened up
like little cushions filled with air
so that you could breathe easily.

Your mother lifted you up in her arms
and held you close.
You looked at her bright eyes and smiling face.
When you came out
the cord still joined you to your placenta.
Then someone cut the cord.
You were breathing all on your own
and no longer needed oxygen from your mother's blood.
Instead, your heart pumped your blood around
inside your body.
The bit of cord that was still on your belly dropped off
when you were about one week old.
It was where your belly button is.

For the first time you felt air on your skin
and you moved your arms and legs
in air instead of water.
There were strange noises.
But in the middle of all the other sounds
was your mother's voice,
one you already knew.
Perhaps she remembers what she said
and how she felt
and how you looked
and what you did.

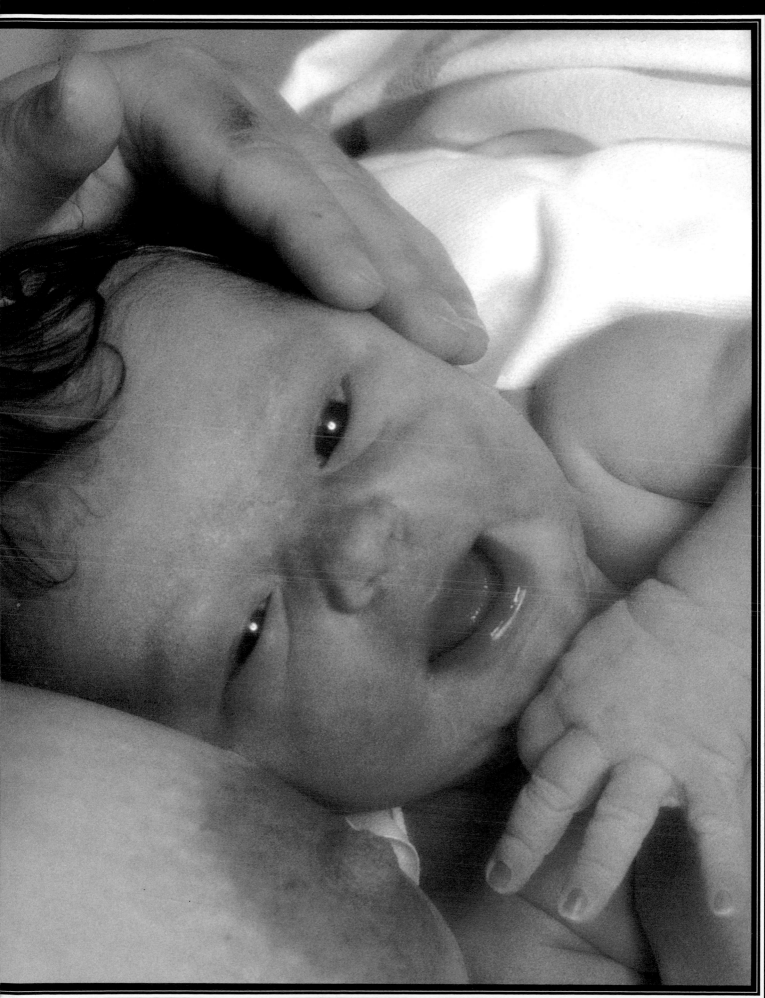

You could see colors and lights
and the curve and shine of things
and the shapes of people's faces smiling at you.
They moved toward you
and away from you.
They were often blurred and fuzzy,
like faces seen through frosted glass
or in a mist.
Only when they came close did you see them clearly.
People touched you
and you could feel hands stroking, cradling,
and holding you.

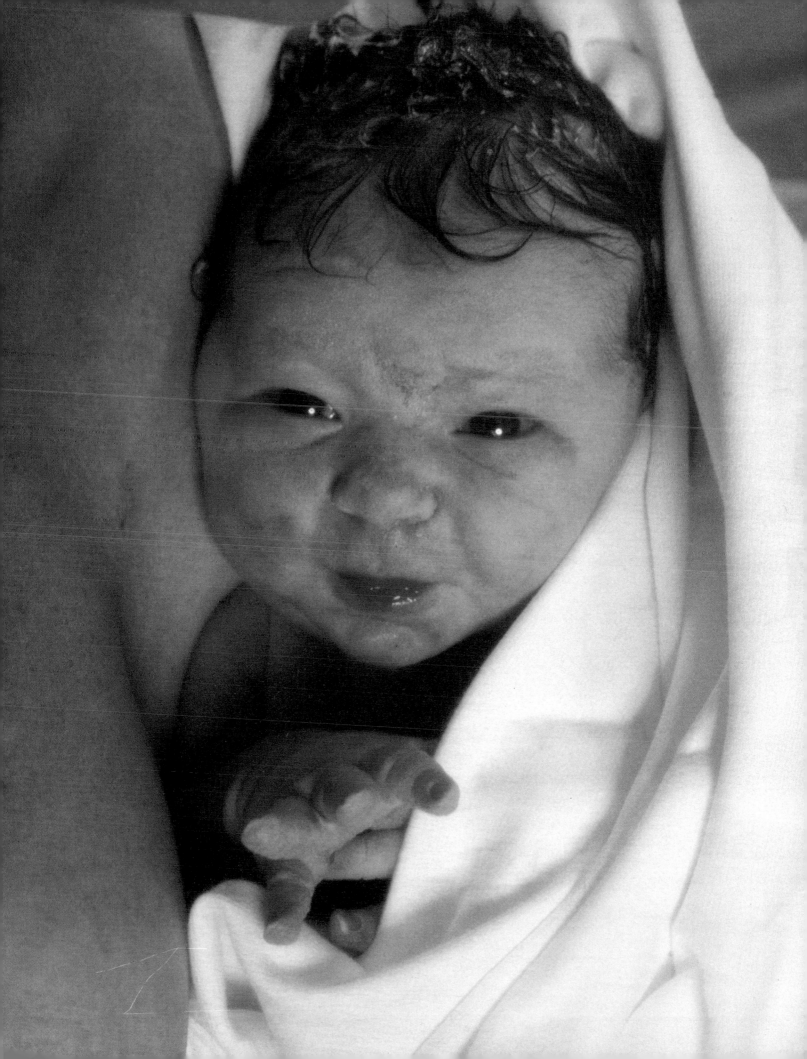

As you lay in your mother's arms
you started to turn your head
and open your mouth
and screw up your eyes
and make funny little mewing noises like a kitten.
You were telling your mother that you wanted to suck.
Already she had milk in her breasts for you.
She lifted you to her breast
and you opened your mouth wide
and latched on.
You sucked and sucked until . . .

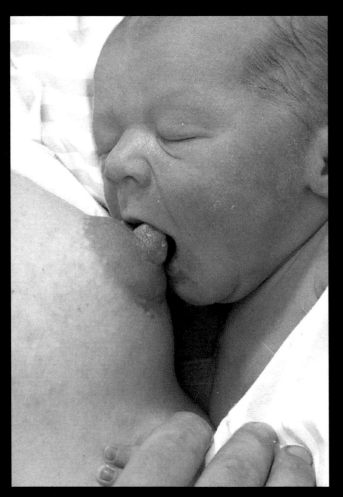
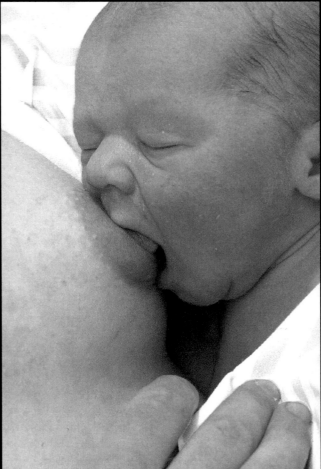

You fell asleep.

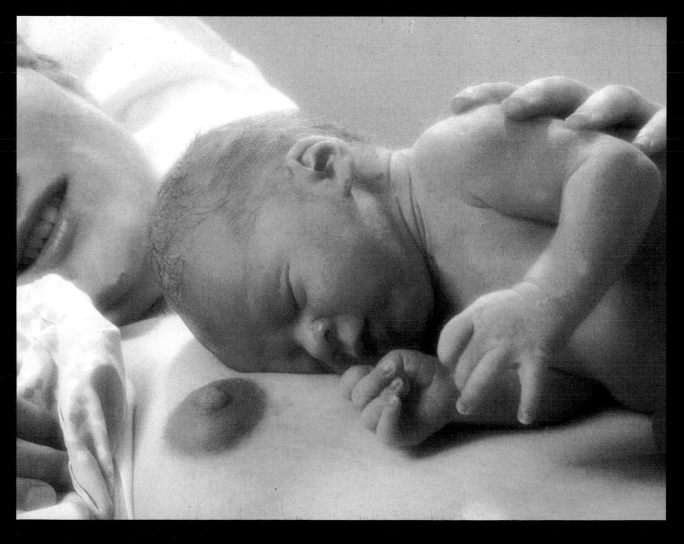

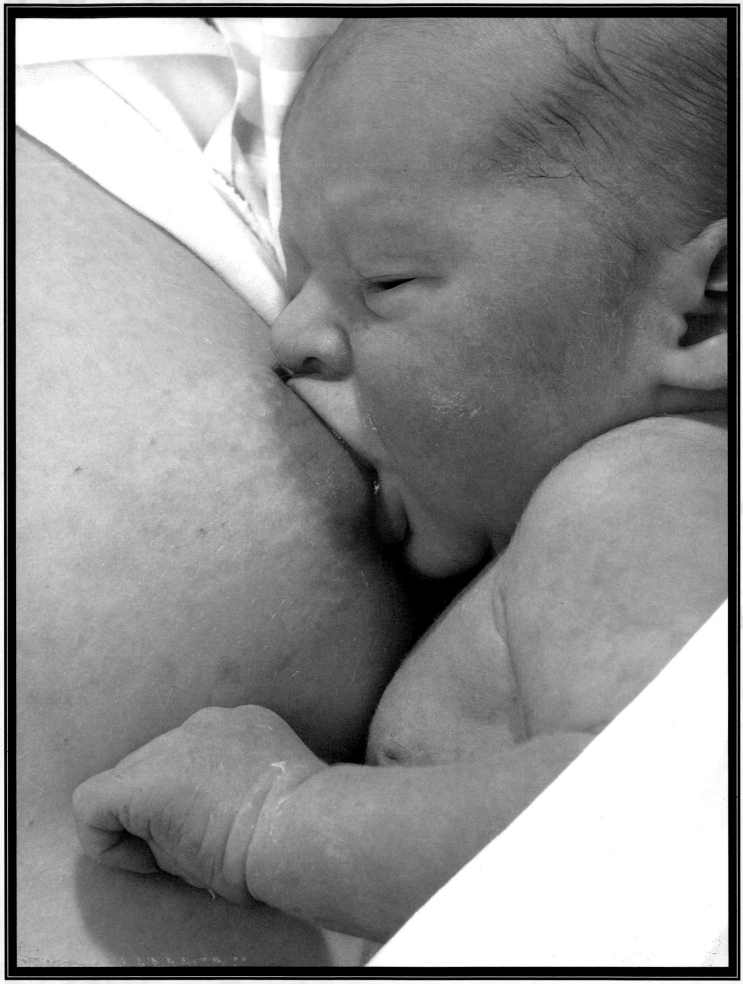